The

ACADIA FILES

Summer Science

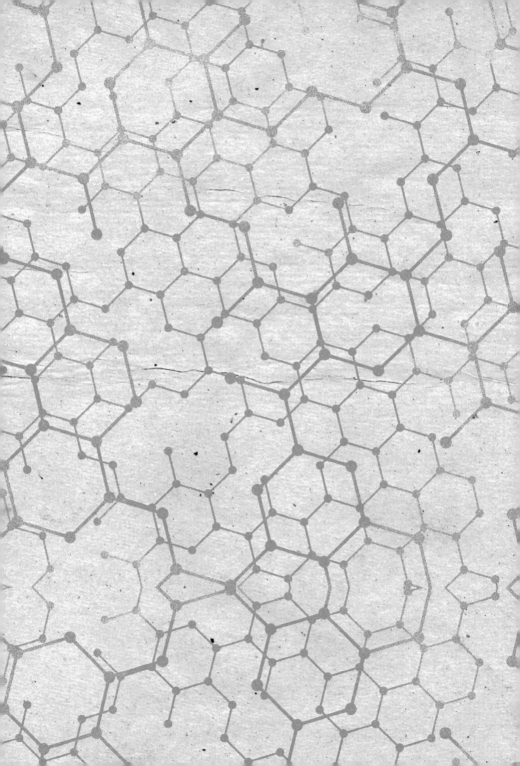

The ACADIA FILES

Summer Science

Katie Coppens

Illustrated and designed by
Holly Hatam

TILBURY HOUSE PUBLISHERS, THOMASTON, MAINE

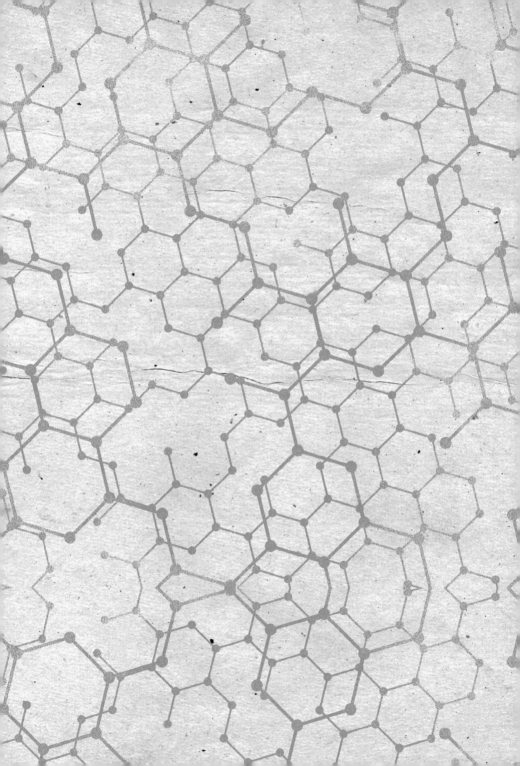

Contents

For those who are curious,
especially Aurea, Iris, and Andrew.
—K.C.

For Mom and Dad, who never
told me to get a real job.
—H.H.

1
The Missing Blueberries

Acadia wakes up to a gentle summer breeze blowing through her window. She puts her messy curls in a ponytail and runs down her house's creaky old stairs.

Acadia dashes past her dad, who is sitting at the kitchen table reading the newspaper. "Morning, Dad!" she hollers as the screen door slams behind her.

She races past her mom, who is watering the vegetable garden, and shouts, "Morning, Mom! I'm going to check on my berries."

"I hope there's enough for blueberry pancakes," Acadia's mom answers with a smile.

Pancakes are a Sunday morning tradition in Acadia's house. She's been waiting to pick her berries until they are so juicy and sweet that they will burst with flavor in her mouth.

As Acadia runs behind the garage to look at her four blueberry bushes, she is thinking that this is the morning when all the work of planting the bushes, watering them on hot summer days, and weeding them will finally pay off. Today is the day she'll get to eat her first handful of delicious blueberries.

"NO!" Acadia shouts as she looks at her bushes.

The family's golden retriever, Baxter, lets out a sharp bark and rushes toward her.

"Acadia, are you okay?" her mom asks as she puts down the garden hose.

Acadia moves from one blueberry bush to the next, chanting, "No, No, No, No, NO!"

With Acadia's final "No!" still echoing through the yard, Acadia's dad opens the porch door.

"Any chance you want to take this one?" Acadia's mom asks.

Acadia's dad nods. Still in his pajamas, he walks toward the blueberry bushes.

"My blueberries are gone! Yesterday I had so many blueberries, and now there are no good ones left. There are only these little ones that are nowhere near ready to be picked." Acadia crawls on her hands and knees, searching for any sign of dark blue on the ground beneath the bushes.

"Here's one," her dad offers, pointing at a blueberry hidden among the leaves.

Without thinking, Acadia picks it off the bush and pops it into her mouth. "Not fair, it's so good. Where'd they all go?" She sits down, puts her head in her hands, then instantly looks up. "I know who did it. It was Joshua."

"Acadia, you don't know that."

"Yes, I do know that. He's so mean."

"Acadia, you have no proof. You can't just accuse someone without—"

"Dad, you know he stole them. He can see the berries from his backyard," Acadia says, pointing to the low split-rail fence.

Acadia's dad sits down beside her. "You can't just accuse someone without evidence."

"How do I get evidence? He ate all the evidence."

"You could start by talking to him about it."

"No way. I'm not talking to him. I have a better idea. I'm going to use my binoculars to watch the bushes. When new blueberries start to grow and he comes to eat them, I'm going to catch him in the act."

"Or you could talk to him."

"And I'm going to paint a sign that says, 'Don't Pick.' That way he's stealing and breaking the law."

"Or you could . . ." her dad says again, but then he pauses, because it's clear that Acadia's mind is set. "Just clean up the paint after you're done."

Acadia stands up and says, "I can't believe him. He ruins everything."

"I know you wanted blueberry pancakes, but how about if I put chocolate chips in them instead? Will that help a little?"

Acadia nods and brushes the dirt off her striped pajamas. Excited about her plan, she rushes past her mom, who is walking toward her. Acadia eagerly walks into the open garage and starts looking for an old wooden board and some bright red paint.

"Acadia, what are you doing?" her mom asks.

I'm going to catch Joshua stealing my berries."

"How could Joshua steal your berries?"

"Um . . . by being his usual horrible self."

"No, I mean how could he steal your berries? Remember, he and his dad are gone for the weekend, hiking Mount Katahdin."

"Then who stole them?" Acadia asks, as she sets down an old piece of wood.

"Why don't you approach this like a scientist and figure out who would eat your berries?"

"What do you mean?"

"Use the scientific method."

Acadia makes a face. "Why do both of my parents have to be science teachers?"

Acadia's mom guides her back toward the bushes and says, "You have a question, so let's see if you can figure out the answer."

"What do you mean, 'use the scientific method?'"

"It's an organized way of answering a question or explaining why something happens. You already have a problem you want to solve, so next you do some research. Then you come up with a hypothesis, and after that—"

"That sounds like a lot of work. I'm just going to paint a sign."

"I'll give you a hint: Whoever it was that ate your berries can't read."

"But there are no little kids in our neighborhood. I don't get it."

"Sit back for a second and observe nature and come up with a hypothesis. It'll help you calm down."

"What's a hypoth—what's that word? Remember, I'm only ten."

"A hypothesis is your best scientific explanation."

"I still can't believe it wasn't Joshua," Acadia mumbles as she walks toward the backyard.

She sits down, leans her hands back into the grass, and looks up at the far-spreading branches of the maple tree. Next, she looks at the row of lilac bushes that are no longer in bloom, then at the beach towels hanging on the clothesline, and finally at her mom's vegetable garden.

She mutters, "I have no idea."

And then Acadia hears a sound echo through the warm morning air—*Chickadee-dee-dee, Chickadee-dee-dee*—and watches a tiny bird fly back and forth between the lilac bushes and the big maple tree. As another round of *Chickadee-dee-dee* begins, the final 'dee' sets off an alarm in her mind.

"Birds! It was birds." She runs to her mom. "I think it was birds!"

"That's a good thought. The birds have probably been watching those berries even more closely than you have. I'm going to guess they woke up early this morning with the same plan that you had, but they beat you to it."

"I can't believe it was the birds," Acadia says, as she looks up at the sky.

"Now that you have a hypothesis, how can you test it to see if it's true?"

"I could cover the berries so the birds can't get to them. If the berries keep growing, that would mean it was birds."

"What could you cover them with?"

"A tarp?" Acadia pictures what the green bushes would look like covered in a big blue tarp. "No, not a tarp. The bushes need sun and water."

"Keep thinking. What don't birds like?"

"They don't like Baxter, but I'm not going to tie him up out there; that would be mean."

Acadia looks into the garage. She sees the workbench, two rakes, bikes, a sled, and sports equipment. She walks over to the sports equipment and yells to her mom, who's picking flowers, "What if I cover them with my soccer goal? It's a net, so sun and water could go through, but I don't think the birds would be able to get to the berries."

"That's good thinking."

Acadia walks toward the bushes holding the soccer net over her head, but pauses until her mom looks up. "I have a better idea. I'm going to cover three bushes but not the fourth. If the bushes under the net have more berries after a week or two than the bush that isn't covered, then I'll know for sure that the net made a difference."

"You just designed an experiment. You're making one change to see if there is a cause and effect. Now, you'll know if your hypothesis is true. But is it okay that birds will probably take berries from that one bush?"

"It wouldn't be okay if it was Joshua, but I'm okay sharing with the birds. After all, now that the birds have tasted my delicious blueberries, it's only fair to let them have a little more. And you know what? I'm going to write about all of this in the notebook you gave me at the start of summer."

"Great idea!"

"Pancakes are ready!" Acadia's dad hollers from the screen door.

Acadia drops the soccer goal and races her mom to the warm, chocolaty stack of pancakes waiting for them on the kitchen table. After breakfast she covers three blueberry bushes with the soccer net, and then she opens her notebook and creates an illustrated "Acadia's Science Notebook" title page. She records her observations three, six, and nine days later, and when the experiment is done, she fills in the next few pages.

The
SCIENTIFIC
METHOD
is loopy

Ask a question

 How?

Do some research

Make a
hypothesis

keep investigating!

Test your
hypothesis

Do the test
results support
your hypothesis?

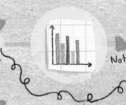 Not yet...

Yes!

Formalize your
Conclusions

Communicate
your results!

BLUEBERRIES DECISION TREE

Question ➤➤➤ Who stole my blueberries ?!

Hypothesis ➤➤➤ JOSHUA (that jerk) ✗   ✓

Evidence ➤➤➤
🟩 Supporting
🟦 Refuting

He's a jerk

Love berries!

Not away for the weekend

Away for the weekend

results of the soccer net experiment!

SKETCH OF MY EXPERIMENT

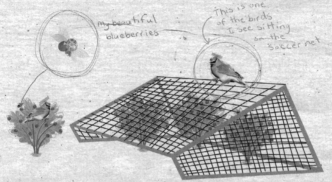

my beautiful blueberries

This is one of the birds I see sitting on the soccer net

Day	Observations of Blueberry Bush with No Soccer Net	Observations of Blueberry Bushes Covered with a Soccer Net
3	I see very few blueberries that are blue. However, there are many berries that are yellowish and light pinkish-blue	There are more blueberries that are blue on these bushes! I also saw birds resting on the frame of the soccer net.
6	A few more pinkish blueberries. I saw a bird fly from the frame of the soccer net to the bush and eat a berry.	There are more blueberries on these bushes. I noticed a bird (my mom called it a cedar waxwing) eating berries between the holes of the net.
9	Just a few blueberries. I noticed a robin on the ground next to the bush.	I continue to see birds on the frame. More blueberries are on the bottom part of the bush than the top.

Conclusion:

I think birds ate the blueberries. The bush without a net around it has the least blueberries. The three bushes with the net around them have more, but still not a lot. Birds like to sit on the soccer net. I think the net's holes are too big. Birds can still get to some of the berries.

NEW SCIENCE WORDS

Scientific Method

A way to find answers to questions you have.

← It's step-by-step

Hypothesis

What you think will happen. It's a smart, scientific prediction.

Your hypothesis may change as you learn more

Evidence

Facts that help you prove something.

PROOF

→ This makes me feel like a detective!

Conclusion

The answer to your question.

It's what you learn!

?!?!

Things I Still Wonder:

- Does the shape of a bird's beak determine if it eats berries?

- Do blueberries taste the same to birds as they do to me? Are all animal taste buds the same?

- What else could keep the birds away besides a net? Maybe a recording of Baxter barking or a stuffed animal of a creature that eats birds, like an owl?

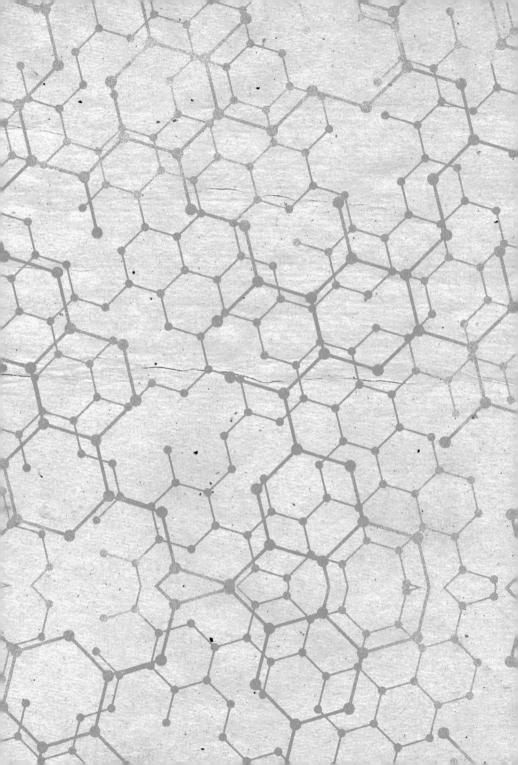

2
It's All About the Genes

One August afternoon, Acadia and her friend Isabel are kicking a soccer ball back and forth in Acadia's backyard.

With each kick of the ball, the girls talk about starting fifth grade and all the things they're going to do in the last few weeks of summer. Trips to the beach are at the top of their list.

"Who's that?" Joshua yells loudly from his side of the low fence.

Joshua is one year younger than Acadia, and his favorite hobby is tormenting her. Acadia has learned that when she ignores him, he eventually gets bored or distracted and leaves her alone.

"I said, who's that?" Joshua yells again, even louder.

Seeing Isabel look over her shoulder at Joshua, Acadia tries to think of something that will make him go away. "Please don't talk to us," she says.

Isabel kicks the soccer ball back to Acadia. "Acadia, be nice," she says. "Hello there, little boy." She then quietly asks Acadia, "Is this the neighbor you always complain about? He's like a kindergartener. How can he be that bad?"

"He's going into the fourth grade. Trust me, don't talk to him."

"Your friend is ginormous," Joshua hollers loudly to Acadia.

"Excuse me?" Isabel picks up the soccer ball and walks toward him. "Did you just call me *ginormous*?"

Acadia runs over to her. "Just walk away and avoid eye contact," she says, tugging on her friend's elbow. "Once he thinks you'll talk to him, he never stops."

"Are you like, part giraffe or something?" Joshua yells. "Why are you so tall?"

"Why are you so small?" Isabel replies. "Are you like, part ant or something?"

Joshua frowns at Isabel. "Oh yeah? Well—"

"Trust me, walk away from him *now*," Acadia whispers, guiding her friend toward the house.

"You're not only part giraffe, you're all giraffe!" Joshua yells as Acadia and Isabel escape in through the back door.

"What is wrong with that boy?" Isabel asks. "At least he didn't say anything mean to you."

"Don't worry, it's not just you. He usually calls me Frizbo."

"Frizbo?" Isabel smiles.

"Because of my curly hair." Acadia looks around the living room and takes a deep breath before yelling, "Mom! Joshua's being mean again!"

"Again?" Acadia's mom sighs. She is stretched out on the couch, reading, just a few feet away. She closes her book and sits up.

"I don't like that boy," Isabel says.

"What did he do?" Acadia's mom asks, motioning for the girls to sit next to her on the couch.

"He said I look like a giraffe because I'm so tall."

"I'm so sorry, Isabel. Joshua tries to get attention in the wrong ways."

"I know I'm tall, but I never knew I was weird looking."

"You're not," Acadia says. She looks at her friend's lovely black hair and big brown eyes. "You have, like, the prettiest hair in our grade. I just found out that I probably need braces. Your teeth are, like, perfect. And . . ."

"Keep going," Isabel prompts, with a smile.

"And, your height makes you an awesome goalie."

"I don't even get why I'm so tall. I'm ten years old and I'm already five feet, five inches tall. I'm almost taller than my mom."

"Think about how tall your dad is. It's all about genes," Acadia's mom says.

"What do my jeans have to do with it?" Isabel looks down at her cut-off jean shorts, mystified.

"No, not the jeans you wear. G-E-N-E-S. Genes are what make us who we are. They come from our parents, and their genes came from their parents, and so on. Genes get passed on."

"So that's why my hair is curly," says Acadia, looking at her mom's curly hair.

"You're lucky," says Isabel. "That's a good thing to get."

"But I got Mom's freckles, too. I hate my freckles."

"What's wrong with freckles?" Acadia's mom asks, touching the faded freckles on her cheek.

Acadia frowns at her. "Dad doesn't have freckles. Why did I get freckles from you?"

"Freckles are an example of a *trait*, a characteristic that can be inherited from one or both parents."

"But I also got some of Dad's traits, like his brown eyes. Is there any pattern to figuring out what you will and won't get?"

"Yes, some traits are considered dominant. Like Isabel's dimples. Isabel, who in your family has dimples?"

"My mom does. I like having the same dimples as her. But my sister doesn't have dimples. How is that possible if having dimples is dominant?"

"Can you two think of how that's possible?"

"Is she really not my sister? I knew it!" Isabel laughs.

Acadia's mom pats Isabel on the shoulder. "She's your sister. Keep thinking."

"Well, my dad doesn't have dimples. That must be part of it."

"Your dad's genes are part of it. But your ancestors' genes, on both sides, matter too."

"Do your grandparents have dimples?" Acadia asks.

"My mom's mom doesn't have dimples, but my grandpa does. Does that matter?"

"It does. Even though your mom has dimples, she carries the gene for having dimples *and* the gene for *not* having dimples. Does anyone in your dad's family have dimples?"

"I don't think so. So that means that my dad only carries the gene for no dimples."

Acadia jumps in. "But your mom carries the gene for having dimples and the gene for not having them, and that's why it's possible for you to have dimples and your sister *not* to have them. So like it or not, she probably *is* your sister."

Isabel smiles and touches the dimples on the sides of her cheeks. "That means I carry the gene for dimples and the gene for no dimples. So someday I might or might not pass on dimples to my kids. Weird."

"Speaking of weird, how come Joshua's so weird? His parents are nice. When parents are nice, shouldn't their kid be nice too?" Acadia asks.

"Joshua is still trying to figure out who he is. We can't change some parts of us—like how tall we're going to be someday—but luckily, who we are on the inside can always change."

"And when will this change happen?" Acadia asks.

"What Joshua said to you, Isabel, was wrong. But—"

"But what, Mom? He's awful!"

"But it's important that we give him the chance to be a good kid, too. Would you two ever let him kick the soccer ball with you?"

"No! He ruins everything."

"I used to act annoying to my sister when she wouldn't play with me," Isabel offers. "I bet he just needs attention."

"But I don't *want* to play with him."

Isabel sighs. "I probably shouldn't have called him an ant," she says.

"Yes, you should have," Acadia insists. "He deserved it."

"I know Joshua's really self-conscious about his height," Acadia's mom suggests. "He's the smallest boy in his grade."

"Well, now Isabel feels bad about her height, too, because of him."

"It's okay. I kind of like that I have my height because of my dad. He got a college scholarship for basketball. Maybe I'll get something good out of it too," Isabel says as she stands up. Then she reaches for Acadia's hand to pull her up from the couch.

"Do you really want to ask him to play with us?" Acadia asks.

"Let's give him a chance."

"Alright, but I'm going to tell him if he does one mean thing, he's going back to his side of the fence."

"I'll come out, too," Acadia's mom says. "If Joshua is unkind again, I'll talk to him."

"Please tell him to be less annoying," Acadia asks as she opens the back door.

"Acadia, I'd like to talk with you first," Acadia's mom says, motioning to the back step. She and Acadia sit down while Isabel walks over to the soccer ball. "We can't control if we have freckles or dimples, but we can control our choices. We can control how we treat people."

Acadia wants nothing more than to be caring like her mom, but sometimes it's just too hard. She feels so frustrated when she's near Joshua.

"Let's show Joshua how to be kind," her mom says.

"You mean kind of annoying?"

"Acadia . . ."

"It was a joke."

"Remember, Joshua looks up to you."

"Mom, he's tiny. He looks up to everyone."

Acadia's mom smiles at her daughter.

Acadia likes making her mom smile. With softness in her voice, she asks, "Mom, Isabel's waiting. Can I please go?"

Acadia's mom gives her a nod.

As Acadia runs over, Isabel kicks her the ball. Instead of kicking it back, Acadia picks it up and walks over to Joshua, who is climbing on the fence. "Joshua, after you apologize to Isabel, would you like to kick with us for a bit?"

"Really?"

Acadia takes a breath and tries to channel her mom's calmness. "Really."

"That's my girl," Acadia's mom whispers.

Joshua hops over the fence and runs to Isabel. "I'm sorry!"

"What are you sorry for?" Isabel asks.

"I'm sorry for being mean."

"Well, you were, and you were quite rude, too, but I accept your apology. And I'm sorry I called you an ant. I shouldn't have said that. The only reason I said it was because you were being so mean."

"I'm sorry I acted like that. Can I play soccer with you and Acadia?"

"Yes, but please don't ever speak to me, or Acadia, like that again."

"I won't."

Acadia looks over at her mom and sees her smile. That makes Acadia smile, too, feeling proud that she is her mother's daughter.

A few days later, while rain falls outside, Acadia opens her science notebook and records what she has learned about genes. After reading a story her mother suggested about Gregor Mendel's experiments with peas, she practices making a Punnett square to predict the chances of a trait being passed from a parent to a child. She learns that most traits are way too complicated to be tracked with Punnett squares! But, luckily, Punnett squares do work for dimples.

Acadia knows now that regardless of what trait you have, whether it's shared with your mom or dad, you have one copy of each gene from each parent. If you have a gene for dimples paired with another gene for dimples, you'll have dimples. If you have a gene for no dimples paired with another gene for no dimples, you won't have dimples. But if you have a gene for dimples paired with a gene for no dimples, you'll still have dimples, because the gene for dimples is a dominant trait.

When she finishes her Punnett square for Isabel's odds of having dimples, it makes sense to Acadia why Isabel has dimples and her sister doesn't. Both Isabel and her sister had a 50 percent chance of getting dimples.

Punnett Square

Isabel's Mom

	D	d
d	Dd	dd
d	Dd	dd

Isabel's Dad

Punnett square for Isabel's dimples.. Isabel and her sister each had a 50% chance of having dimples.

My Family's Traits

Data on My Family's Traits.
Freckles and dimples can be
mapped with Punnett squares.
Other traits are too complicated
to map this way.

Trait	Me	Mom	Dad
Eye Color	Brown	Blue	Brown
Hair Color	Blonde	Dark Blonde	Brown
Hair Curliness	Yes	Yes	No
Freckles	Yes	Yes	No
Dimples	No	No	No
Can Roll Tongue	Yes	No	Yes
Attached Earlobes	Yes	Yes	Yes
Widow's Peak	No	No	No

NEW SCIENCE WORDS

Genetics

The study of genes.

Genes

The parts of you that come from your relatives. Each gene is a piece of your DNA. Your genes are coded instructions for how your body develops.

Super, super zoomed in

DNA in a cell

DNA

The instruction manual or map for who you are. This map is in all of your cells and includes genes for your eye color, how tall you are, whether you have dimples, and other traits.

Dominant Traits

Traits that are more likely to be passed on.

Recessive Traits

Traits that are less likely to be passed on to you by your ancestors.

Things I Still Wonder:

- If I had a sibling, what traits would he or she have?

- What dog traits are dominant or recessive? I wonder if Baxter looks more like his mom or dad.

- Hmmm... Maybe there is a pun gene? My dad always makes jokes with puns, but I don't find them funny. Maybe I should make a Punnett square and see if telling puns is dominant or recessive? (Just Kidding.)

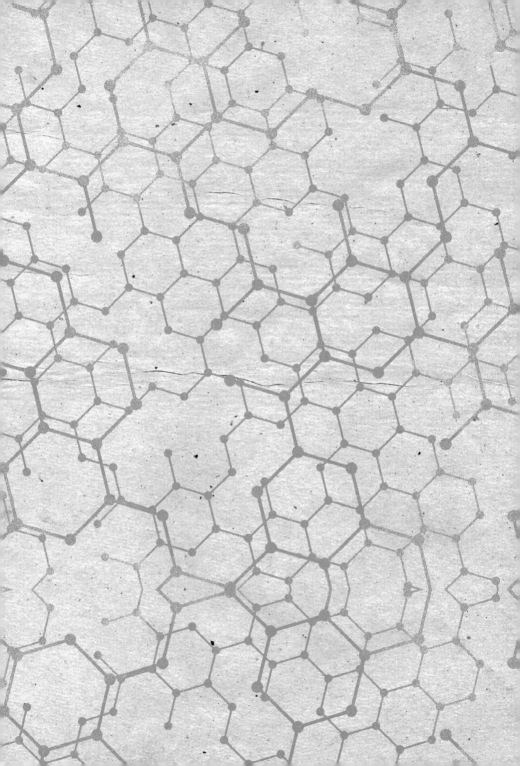

Acadia closes the car door and looks at the bright blue sky that seems to go on forever. The sun shines down on the ocean, causing the crashing waves to glisten.

Acadia and her mom walk on a path of uneven rocks that leads to the sandy beach. Acadia looks like a small shadow of her mom, with the same blonde, curly hair pulled back in a ponytail that bounces with each step.

Looking down at the rocks below, Acadia says, "These rocks are hard to walk on."

Acadia's mom walks with careful steps. She pauses for a moment and says, "Look, Acadia, it's a wishing stone."

Acadia picks up the smooth stone. It's light-gray but has a thin band of white near the center. She turns the stone over in her palm, tracing the white band all the way around it with a finger. Every time Acadia goes to the beach with her parents, they search for stones to skip across the ocean's surface while making a wish.

"Here's another one, Mom!" Acadia picks up a smooth stone and rubs it in each hand as they move toward the sandy part of the beach.

Acadia's mom points to a patch of sand that is big enough for their blanket. "How's this spot?"

"Looks good to me. The sand is soft. That's all I care about." Acadia drops her beach bag on the sand and hands her mom the wishing stones. Acadia takes off her flip-flops and digs her toes into the gritty sand. "How can the ground go from sharp rocks to soft sand, all in a minute-long walk?"

"Let's go down to the water and see if you can figure it out."

Acadia grabs her flip-flops. "I'm bringing these just in case there are rough rocks again."

"Don't worry, there won't be."

"How do you know that?" Acadia asks as she sets her flip-flops down again.

"You'll see. Sea glass will help it make more sense. Will you help me find some?"

"Okay!" Acadia shouts, running ahead. Swimming, building sandcastles, and looking for sea glass are her three favorite things to do at the beach.

After walking for a minute, Acadia notices a piece of frosted white sea glass close to the high tide line. Crouching down to pick up the smooth, white glass, she also grabs a handful of sand and looks at the mix of colors and textures. Most of the sand is soft and brown, but some grains look like tiny crystals, while others are like small flecks of black coal.

She continues to walk, then sees a brown piece of sea glass that blends in with the seaweed that's scattered over the shore. This piece of glass has just started to become worn down and does not yet have the frosted look of the white piece. She runs back to her mom, who has two pieces in her hand, one frosted green and one clear and sharp as if it has just broken off a soda bottle.

"Can you line these pieces up by how smooth they are?" Acadia's mom asks.

Acadia holds up the sharp piece of clear glass. "We should throw this one back in the water or maybe even in the trashcan. It's not really sea glass yet. Mom, you pretty much just picked up someone's trash."

"Hey, hold on. I picked it up for a reason. I want to see if you can figure this out. The pieces of glass are like rocks in a way, and they can answer your question about why some rocks are rough and some are smooth."

Acadia looks at the sea glass, then at the sharp rocks in the distance. "I don't get it."

"Well, how does sea glass form?"

"From being rough like this," Acadia says, pointing at the sharp glass, "to smooth and frosted."

"How does that happen?"

"Waves hit the broken glass against rocks and sand and it gets smoother." Acadia looks at her mom, who raises an eyebrow. Acadia knows a raised eyebrow means she's close to figuring something out. She looks at the rough rocks far above the high tide line, then down at the soft sand at the shoreline. "The same thing happens with rocks! That's why the closer we get to the water, the smoother the rocks get. Waves smooth down the rocks by pounding against them."

"Exactly. So what do you think sand is?" Acadia's mom points to the wet sand that is being pushed and pulled by the incoming tide.

Acadia scoops up a handful of wet sand, then feels a cold splash of water run across her feet. A wave washes gritty sand and broken seashells over her toes. A moment later, the water retreats to the sea. A few seconds later, her feet are buried again by another wave. Acadia imagines what it would feel like to be a rock with waves, sand, and shells hitting her again and again, for hours, days, weeks, years.

As the next wave comes, Acadia smiles at her mom. "I think sand was once part of bigger rocks. Just like how that piece of glass was once from a bottle. As waves pound rocks and sand against other rocks they wear it down. The rocks break down and get smoother over time. That's why it's sandy by the water."

Acadia's mom smiles at her daughter and picks up a handful of sand. "See all the different colors? Can you figure out why the sand doesn't all look the same?"

Acadia touches the sand. The clear sand, black sand, and brown sand all have different textures. Some pieces are smooth like glass, and others are coarse like sandpaper. She thinks about the rough rocks she walked over earlier, and how each one was unique. When she looks closely at the sand, each grain looks like a really, really small rock. "They look different because they are from different types of rocks. Just like pieces of sea glass have different colors because they come from different types of bottles."

"You got it."

"So if I throw a rock in the water, someday it could wear down into millions of pieces of sand."

"A long time from now."

"That's amazing."

Acadia's mom reaches into her pocket and takes out the two wishing stones. "But for now, let's appreciate these," she says, handing one to Acadia.

"It took a long time for those stones to become so smooth," Acadia says. "Now I get why they're called wishing stones. They are really, really special. But how did this gray stone get a white stripe?"

"Ah," says her mother, looking closely at the rock. "A rock is formed when different minerals compress or melt together. Some rocks contain lots of minerals, but this rock looks like it contains just feldspar and quartz. The gray is feldspar, and the white band going through it is quartz. Quartz can make veins in rocks and minerals when they form."

Acadia slowly rubs her thumb over her stone and silently makes a wish before skipping it across the glistening blue water. Later, when they get home, her mom opens a box containing several kinds of rocks and minerals. She gives three pieces of mica and four pieces of quartz to Acadia. Examining the minerals, Acadia comes up with an idea for an experiment based on what she learned at the beach. Before she knows it, this idea leads to more questions. Acadia's mom says that the answers to science questions always raise more questions. That's how scientists discover new things.

My Mineral Experiment

My question: Do some rocks break down more easily than others? Rocks are made of minerals, so does that mean that some minerals break down more easily than others?

Research: Unlike rocks, minerals are pure all the way through. The mineral quartz is just quartz, whereas a rock can be made up of several minerals. For example, granite is a rock made up of the minerals quartz, feldspar, and mica.

I found out there is something called the Mohs scale of mineral hardness, which ranks minerals by how hard they are. For example, talc is a 1 (least hard) and diamond is a 10 (hardest). A harder mineral can scratch a softer one. A diamond can scratch talc very easily. Mica is a 2.5 on the Mohs scale, and quartz is a 7.

Hypothesis: If I put pieces of quartz in one container, pieces of mica in another container, and shake both containers for the same amount of time, the mica will break apart more because it's not as hard as quartz.

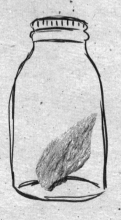
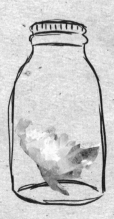

Procedure:

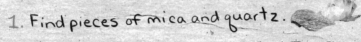
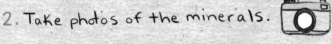

1. Find pieces of mica and quartz.

2. Take photos of the minerals.

3. Put the samples of mica in a plastic container with a screw-on lid.

4. Put the samples of quartz in another plastic container with a screw-on lid.

5. Hold one container in one hand and one container in the other hand and shake them 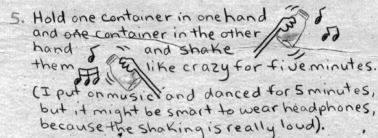 like crazy for five minutes.

   (I put on music and danced for 5 minutes, but it might be smart to wear headphones, because the shaking is really loud).

6. Put on safety goggles.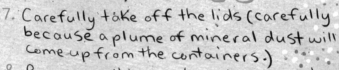

7. Carefully take off the lids (carefully because a plume of mineral dust will come up from the containers.)

8. Pour everything out and observe how much the minerals broke down.

9. Take photos of the minerals.

10. Compare the "before" photos with the "after" photos to see the difference.

Materials: A few samples of two types of minerals, two plastic containers with screw-on lids, safety goggles, headphones, camera.

mica

quartz

Safety First!

safety goggles

containers

Awesome pink headphones!

Camera

Say cheese!

Data from My Mineral Experiment

Mineral	Photograph Before Shaking for 5 Minutes	Photograph After Shaking for 5 minutes
Mica		
Quartz		

Conclusion: This experiment was like high-speed mechanical weathering. After just 5 minutes of shaking, the mica broke down a lot. It went from three large pieces to many pieces (there are way too many pieces to count). The edges of the mica and quartz smoothed down. The quartz did not change as much as the mica did. There are still four large pieces of quartz. I count 14 tiny pieces of quartz that broke off, and I see lots of soft, powdery quartz sand. This experiment helped me understand why there are so many little pieces of mica on Maine's beaches; it breaks down really easily.

Rocks break down through weathering

waves

animals

roots

ice

water gets in crack and expands when it freezes

gravity

Rocks broken by weathering might slide downhill, like in a landslide, which can break them down more.

NEW SCIENCE WORDS

Weathering

When rocks wear down over time. It's caused by movement or chemicals.

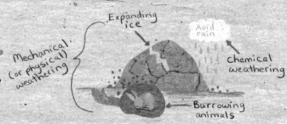

Mechanical (or physical) weathering

Expanding ice

Acid rain

Chemical weathering

Burrowing animals

Sediment

Small pieces of broken off rock. Grains sometimes are small (like sand) or large (like a pebble) depending on the amount of weathering.

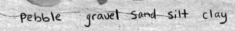

Pebble   gravel   sand   silt   clay

Erosion

When rock or sediment is carried from one place to another by wind, water, ice or gravity. A sandstorm is an example of wind erosion. A gully is formed by water erosion.

Deposition

Where the rock or sediment lands.

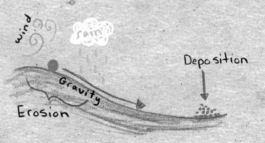

wind

rain

Deposition

Gravity

Erosion

Things I Still Wonder:

- How do minerals form? Does the way they form impact how hard they are?

- If I put the quartz in the container with the mica, would the mica have broken down even more because quartz is harder than mica?

- Are diamonds so expensive because they are a 10 on the Mohs hardness scale?

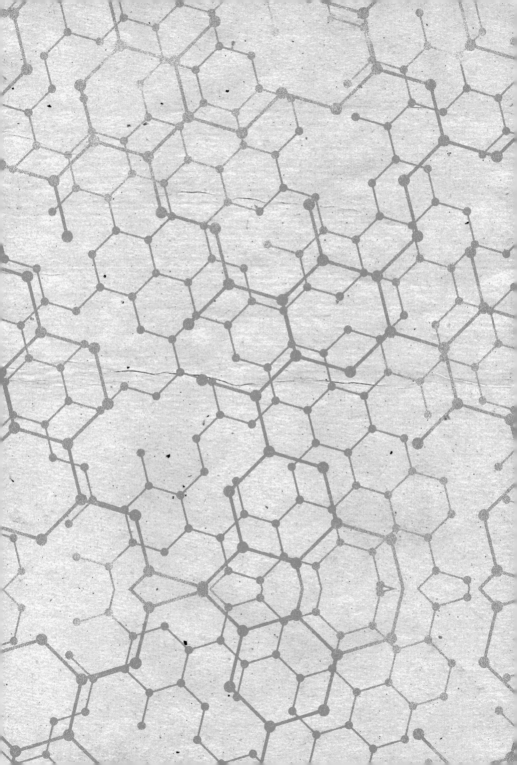

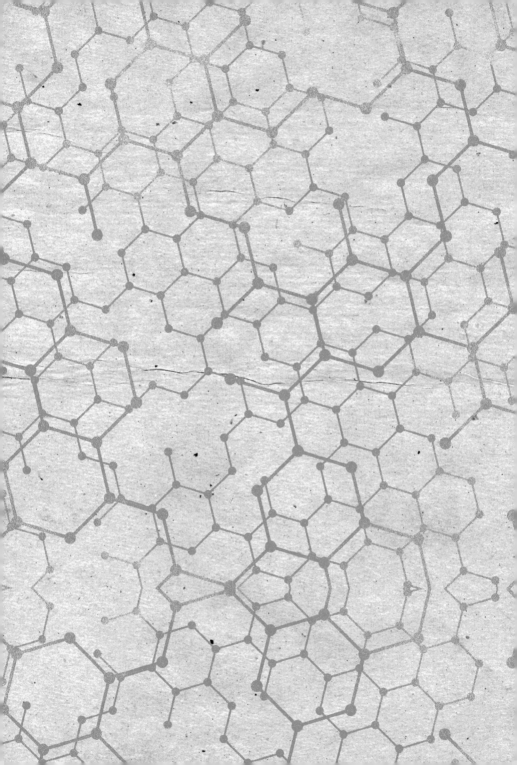

Acadia groans as the early morning light shines through her bedroom window. She rolls away from the sun, pulling the sheet tightly over her head. As she reaches for a pillow to block out more light, she hears the birds chirping again and again. It's as if they are having a long, excited conversation about something. Most likely it's about eating Acadia's delicious blueberries. Acadia pulls back the sheets and yells, "Please go back to sleep!"

Just at that moment Acadia's dad is downstairs sipping his morning cup of coffee. With Acadia's yell still echoing through the house, he puts down his coffee mug and runs upstairs. Opening Acadia's bedroom door, he sees her hair peeking out from the sheets.

"Acadia, are you okay?" he asks.

Acadia shakes her head and buries herself deeper under the covers. "No," she moans from beneath the sheets. "I'm being picked on."

"Who's picking on you? Is it Joshua? I thought things were getting better between the two of you—"

"It's not Joshua. It's the sun. *And* the birds." Acadia peels back the sheet, revealing furrowed eyebrows and a freckled, frustrated face. "Isn't it enough that I'm letting them eat my blueberries? Now, they won't let me sleep. Will you close the window and shut the curtains for me?"

"You should've done that before you went to bed. You know the sun's going to come up."

"It's summer. Why does the sun have to come up so early when I finally get to sleep in?" Acadia asks as she sits up.

"Do you want to know why the sun is up so early, or would you rather sleep?"

"I'm awake. I might as well understand why I'm awake so early."

Acadia's dad reaches for the stuffed bear that rests beside Acadia. "Let me show you why you shouldn't blame the sun. Let's pretend Bob here is Earth. Actually, let's just pretend his head is Earth."

Acadia yawns and rubs her eyes.

"*Bear* with me," he says with a smile. "And yes, my dear, that was a pun before six-thirty in the morning."

Acadia smiles and shakes her head at her dad's joke. She likes to tease him about his puns, but she does love his corny humor.

Acadia's dad leans over to pick up a soccer ball from the floor. "Now, let's pretend your soccer ball here is the sun. Can you get Earth to orbit around the sun?"

Acadia takes Bob and moves him in an arc around the soccer ball.

"Good, but you forgot something. Earth is constantly spinning while it orbits."

Acadia starts the orbit again, this time spinning the bear in a full 360-degree turn while it orbits.

"What do you notice?" Acadia's dad asks.

Acadia sees how Bob faces the sun, then turns away from it. Then he turns to face the sun again. "I get it. If Earth didn't spin, only half the planet would get sunlight.

One side of the planet would always be in the dark." Acadia spins Bob and thinks about her day. It's light when she wakes up, then dark when she goes to bed. When she wakes up, it's light again. "It must take one day for Earth to make a full rotation on its axis."

"Yes, it takes 24 hours. That's why we have 24 hours in a day."

"But I still don't get it. Why is there more sunlight in the summer than in the winter?"

"You see how you're holding Bob straight up and down? Earth is actually at an angle. It's a 23.5-degree angle, which means— "

"We're tilted . . ." Acadia angles Bob's head toward the soccer ball. "So, us being tilted toward the sun has something to do with it." Acadia moves Bob around the soccer ball, keeping him at a slight angle like he's about to head the ball. She notices that when he's on the other side of the soccer ball, the part of his head that was angled toward the sun is now angled away from it.

"Right now we're angled toward the sun," Acadia's dad hints. "So this must mean . . ."

"When we're tilted toward the sun, it's summer, and when we're tilted away from the sun it's winter," Acadia finishes. Then, she realizes something else. When the top part of Bob's head is angled toward the sun, the bottom part is angled away. "So right now it's summer for us, but it's winter on the lower half of Earth."

Acadia's dad smiles. "We call that the southern hemisphere. So when it's winter here . . ."

"It's summer there."

"You got it! When one half of Earth is tilted toward the sun, the other half is tilted away. If we weren't tilted, we wouldn't have changing seasons."

"That would be so boring!"

Then Acadia thinks of something else. She moves Bob to the point in his orbit halfway between where the top of his head tilts directly toward the ball and where it tilts directly away. "What about here, Dad?" she asks. "Now neither half of Earth is tilted toward the sun. What is this called?"

"It's the spring equinox in the northern hemisphere, halfway from winter to summer. And it's the autumn equinox in the southern hemisphere, halfway from summer to winter."

Acadia nods. "Can you hand me my notebook and pencil?" she asks.

As she starts to draw in her notebook, she thinks of another question. "But not everyone has seasons like us. How is that possible?"

"If you live close to the equator, an imaginary line around the middle of Earth halfway between the poles, the tilt doesn't affect you very much, so the amount of daylight stays pretty much the same. But we live in Maine, which is about halfway from the equator to the north pole, so the tilt affects us a lot."

Acadia points to the ears on the top of Bob's head. "What about people who live up here?"

"People in the far north have very long, dark winters. In Fairbanks, Alaska, on December 21, the sun is only above the horizon for four hours in the middle of the day. In Nome, way up in northern Alaska, the sun doesn't come up at all from late November to late January. But on June 21, the sun's above the horizon for 21 hours in

Fairbanks, and in Nome it doesn't set at all from early May until early August."

"How do you know so much, Dad, and more importantly, how do people in Alaska sleep in the summer?"

"They buy really thick curtains to block out the light."

"I think I need some of those." Acadia gets up and pulls her curtains tightly closed. She hops back into bed and closes her eyes. "Thanks, Dad. I don't hate the sun anymore."

A loud *Chickadee-dee-dee* echoes through Acadia's room from a bird outside.

"Now if only I could understand those birds," Acadia sighs, pulling a sheet over her head. Then she pops out again. "Wait! I do understand the birds! They are probably annoyed that the sun woke them up, too."

"You know what they say, the early bird gets the . . ."

"Blueberries?" Acadia smiles.

"I was going to say worm, but yes, I suppose they get your blueberries too."

"Just save some for me, birds. Save some for me," Acadia says, as she rolls over and goes back to sleep.

When Acadia wakes up two hours later, she opens her curtains to a beautiful, sunny day. She sees the maple tree's long shadow in her yard and thinks about what her dad taught her about Earth's rotation on its axis and its orbit around the sun.

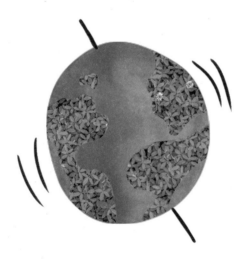

My question: Will the position of the sun in the sky affect the length of my dad's shadow?

Research: In order to make a shadow you need light and something that blocks the light. Because Earth is constantly rotating, the sun moves across the sky.

Hypothesis: If I measure Dad's shadow with the sun in three different locations in the sky, then the higher the sun is in the sky, the shorter Dad's shadow will be.

Procedure:
1. Make sure it is a sunny day.
2. Take Dad (or someone else) outside and have him stand in the driveway with the sun behind him, which will cause a shadow to form in front of him.
3. Use chalk to draw the shape of his shadow.

Oops! This kind of looks like a crime scene!

4. After tracing the shadow, measure its length and record the data.
5. Repeat with the sun at different locations in the sky. (Dad reminded me to be safe; you should never look directly at the sun, even while wearing sunglasses, because it can damage your eyes.)

Materials:

- Sunny day
- chalk
- measuring tool
- Dad or similar person

So many colors to choose from! :)

My dad... I ♥ him

Data:

Time of Day and Location of Sun	Observations	Sketch of Dad's Shadow
7a.m.: Sun is low in the sky, just above eastern horizon	Really Long Shadow!!! 6.12 meters long (20 feet long)	
12 noon: Sun is high in the sky	Short Shadow 1.27 meters long (4 feet, 2 inches long)	
3p.m.: Sun is between the western horizon and the most overhead point in the sky	Medium Shadow 2.86 meters long (9 feet, 5 inches long)	

Conclusion: My hypothesis was correct!!

Dad's shadow was the shortest when the sun was the highest in the sky. I think this happened because the sun was almost directly over his head. The angle of the sun high in the sky compared to Dad straight below led to a much shorter shadow than at other times of the day.

The closer the sun is to the horizon, the longer the shadow will be. It's really cool to make a shadow that is over three times your height!

Earth takes 24 hours to make one rotation

Bob's head = Earth

Daytime is when we <u>face</u> the sun

Nighttime is when we face away from the sun

I need sunglasses!

It's daytime on the other side of the Earth

We have seasons because of the Earth's tilt

imaginary axis that Earth spins around

Earth has a 23.5° tilt

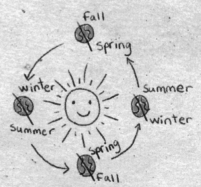

fall

spring

winter

summer

summer

winter

spring

fall

NEW SCIENCE WORDS

One complete revolution around the sun takes one year... 365 days!

orbit

Revolution

Earth orbiting around the sun.

Earth

Elliptical

The path of Earth's orbit around the sun is not a perfect circle.

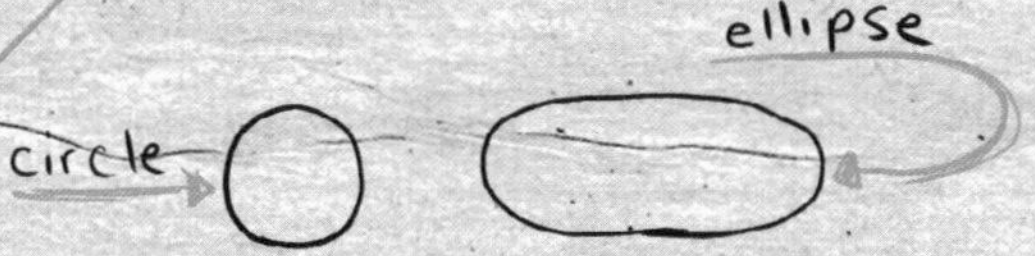

circle

ellipse

Rotation

Spinning

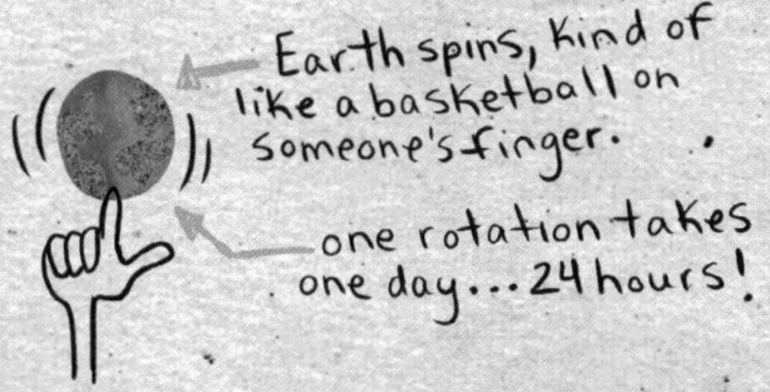

Earth spins, kind of like a basketball on someone's finger.

one rotation takes one day... 24 hours!

Axis

Tilt

Earth spins on an axis, which is at a 23.5 degree tilt

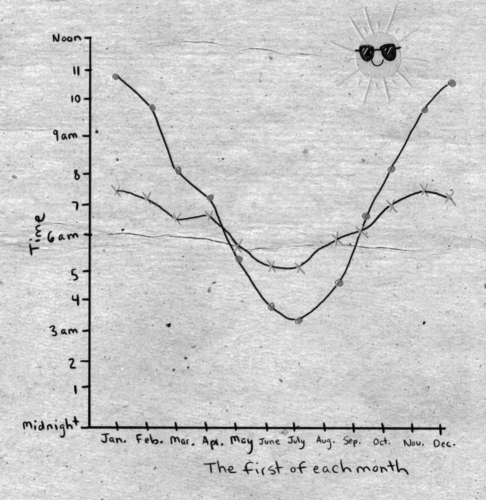

Sunrise times for Freeport, Maine and Fairbanks, Alaska

The first of each month

Key:
X = Freeport, ME
O = Fairbanks, AK

Things I Still Wonder:

- How does a sundial work? I noticed the direction of a shadow changes depending on where the sun is. If Dad had stayed in the same position all day, would he have been a human sundial?
- Do shadows look different in different parts of the world because of Earth's tilt? For example, would Dad's shadow be a different shape and length in Alaska and Maine? (Maybe someday we'll travel to Alaska and find out!)
- I made these measurements on August 15. If I repeat this on November 15, will Dad's shadow be longer at noon because the sun will be lower in the sky then? (New hypothesis: Yes, it will be!)

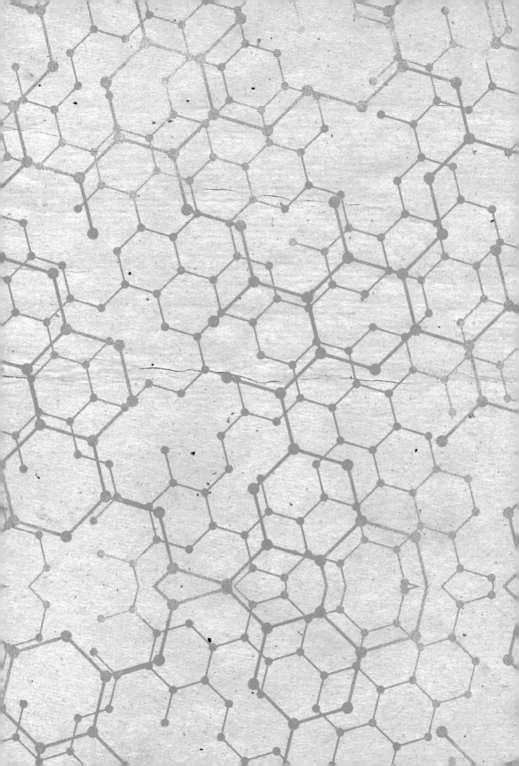

One warm August day, Acadia and Isabel put the final touches on a sandcastle they have spent the last hour building. Acadia places a piece of green sea glass on top of the sandcastle's tallest tower and stands back to admire their work. She motions for her dad to come over. "Can you take a picture of this, Dad? It's our best sandcastle of the summer."

"Too bad the tide's coming up," Isabel says, looking at the water that is less than ten feet away.

"No!" Acadia groans. "We should've built it higher up on the beach. I forgot about the tide."

"But this is where the sand's wet. It makes the best castles," Isabel says.

"You're right. The waves make the sand extra soft here, too," Acadia adds.

Acadia's dad takes out his cell phone and motions the girls toward the sandcastle. "You know when you build a sandcastle that it's temporary. But I'll get a picture. That'll last."

Isabel and Acadia crouch next to the sandcastle and smile for a picture. Acadia's dad holds up his phone and says, "Okay, say 'lunar pull.'"

Acadia giggles. "Why would we say lunar poo?"

"No, silly, I said 'lunar pull.'"

"What are you talking about, Dad?"

"Nothing. Okay, then, say cheese. No, say 'moon cheese.'"

Acadia smiles for the picture, then asks, "Why were you talking about the moon?"

"Because the moon is why we have tides."

Acadia points to the sky. "How can the moon, way up there, have anything to do with our tides down here?"

"Amazingly, it does. The moon has a gravitational pull on Earth, and Earth has a gravitational pull on the moon."

"A gravi-*what*?" Acadia asks.

"A gravitational pull," her dad repeats. "Earth's gravitational pull is what keeps the moon in orbit around Earth. The more mass an object has—and the closer it is—the more gravitational pull the object has."

"In kid words, please?" Acadia asks.

Isabel jumps in. "Oh wait, I know about gravity. It's what keeps us on the ground instead of floating off into space. Gravity is why, when we drop something, it falls down."

"That's right, Isabel," says Acadia's dad. "Objects we drop will always fall toward the center of the Earth, thanks to Earth's gravitational pull. And to us, here on the surface of the planet, 'toward the center of the Earth' means 'down.'"

"How does this connect to tides?" Acadia asks.

"Earth and the moon are kind of like two magnets," Isabel says to Acadia. "You know how, if you put two magnets close, they pull toward each other?"

Acadia's dad adds, "Yes, but picture Earth as a bigger magnet than the moon, because Earth has much more mass."

Isabel says, "The moon pulls at Earth, and Earth pulls at the moon. It's kind of like a tug-of-war. But the poor moon is so much smaller than Earth. It keeps trying, but it will never win."

"Nice analogy, Isabel!" Acadia's dad says. "They both have a gravitational pull on each other. Earth's gravitational pull is so strong that it causes the moon to orbit around us. The moon's gravitational pull causes Earth's oceans to bulge out toward the moon."

Acadia looks at the water. "Wait, Dad, what do you mean by 'bulge'? And more importantly, Isabel, how do you know so much?"

Isabel answers, "My grandparents have a boat, so we need to understand the tides. I know that the moon can pull at Earth's water, but I don't really get what your dad means by the moon causing the water to 'bulge.'"

Acadia's dad says, "Earth's gravitational pull wants to hold the water where it is. But the moon's pull creates a bulge in the water, and this is high tide. The moon pulls most strongly on the oceans that are closest to it, and least strongly on those that are farthest away. The water that faces the moon bulges, and another bulge happens in the water that is facing away from the moon on the far side of Earth."

Acadia's dad bends down and uses his finger to draw a picture in the sand. He draws one circle for Earth and a smaller circle for the moon. Then he adds an oval around his drawing of Earth to represent water. He says, "We have two high tides here in Maine, because the ocean here experiences a bulge of water—a high tide—twice a day as we rotate. When we are not in a bulge, the tide is low."

"I'm starting to get this. But how come the times of high and low tides change each day?" Acadia asks.

"Because both Earth and the moon are moving. The moon orbits around Earth, and Earth orbits around the sun."

"While tilted at a 23.5-degree angle on its axis," Acadia adds.

"Good memory. Because Earth and the moon are moving, the time of the tides changes a little each day. Here in Maine, about twelve and a half hours passes from one high tide to the next or from one low tide to the next. So, if low tide was at 2 a.m., then the next low tide would be around 2:30 p.m. If high tide was at 8 a.m., then the next high tide would be—"

"Hold on, the next high tide would be around . . . 8:30 p.m.," Acadia interjects.

"You're getting it! Maybe we should take another picture to celebrate the thinking both of you are doing. This may be more impressive than the sandcastle."

"I think I get why you said lunar poo now," Acadia teases.

Acadia's dad smiles. "Well, I don't want to confuse you, but the sun has a part in it too."

"What does the sun have to do with it?" Acadia asks.

"Isabel, you had good thinking about this. Can you figure it out?"

"Um, I know the sun is really, really big." Isabel crouches down and adds a large sun to the drawing in the sand, far away from the moon and Earth. "Even though it's far away, I'm guessing it has a gravitational pull on Earth too, and is part of the tug-of-war on the oceans."

"You got it!" Acadia's dad says. "In fact, when the sun, moon, and Earth all line up, we get the biggest tides."

Isabel says, "That makes sense. It's like the moon gets a little help in the tug-of-war!"

A wave crashes at Acadia's feet. "All that is interesting, but what really matters is that the tide is about to wash away our sandcastle." She watches a wave push and pull at the sandcastle and start to break it apart.

"That's okay. Tomorrow's the last day of summer vacation, so now we have an excuse to come back and make another one," Isabel says.

"So the tide isn't all bad, right?" Acadia's dad asks.

"Nope, the tide isn't bad," Isabel says, as she rescues the piece of green sea glass from the top of the sandcastle.

Acadia looks up at the sky and says, "Keep tugging, Moon!"

Her dad smiles. "There you go, Acadia!"

"Well, the tide does make for great swimming!" Acadia takes Isabel's hand and they run toward the waves, laughing.

Tides

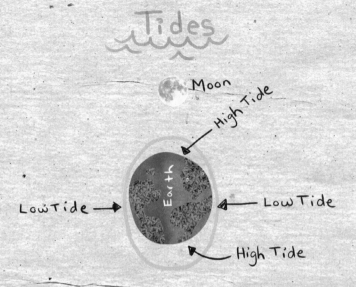

Moon

High Tide

Earth

Low Tide ➝

← Low Tide

High Tide

The phases of the moon impact tides too!

New

Young

Waxing Crescent

Waxing Quarter

Waxing Gibbous

New and full have bigger tides

Full

Waning Gibbous

Waning Quarter

Waning Crescent

Old

Why do new and full moons make bigger tides?

Because at new moon the moon is directly between the Sun and Earth, and at full moon the Earth is directly between the sun and moon. Either way, the sun and moon are aligned, so their gravitational pulls work together to tug on Earth's oceans.

NEW SCIENCE WORDS

Gravity

The force that pulls objects towards one another

Apple falling from the tree to the ground

Gravitational Pull

The size of the force (or pull) caused by gravity. This is impacted by the size of the object and how far away it is (distance).

Distance

The sun is way bigger than the moon, but the moon has a bigger impact on our tides because it's so close to us.

Earth

Moon

Force

The strength of the pull.

small magnets

less → ← force

large magnets

MORE ⇒⇐ FORCE

This Week's Tide Chart for Higgins Beach:

Day	HIGH AM	PM	LOW AM	PM	MOON
Mon.	9:18	9:50	3:03	3:37	
Tues.	10:08	10:37	3:53	4:24	
Wed.	10:57	11:24	4:42	5:10	
Thurs.	11:46		5:32	5:57	
Fri.	12:11	12:37	6:23	6:46	
Sat.	1:00	1:30	7:15	7:37	
Sun.	1:52	2:26	8:11	8:31	

What happened on Thursday?

There was only one high tide because 11:46am is so close to noon. Each high and low tide is 12 hours and almost 30 minutes apart. The next high tide was the next day at 12:11 AM.

Things I Still Wonder:

- Why do some parts of the world only have one high tide in a day, when most have two?

- Why do some planets have lots of moons, others have no moons, and Earth has one moon? If we had more than one moon, what would our tides be like?

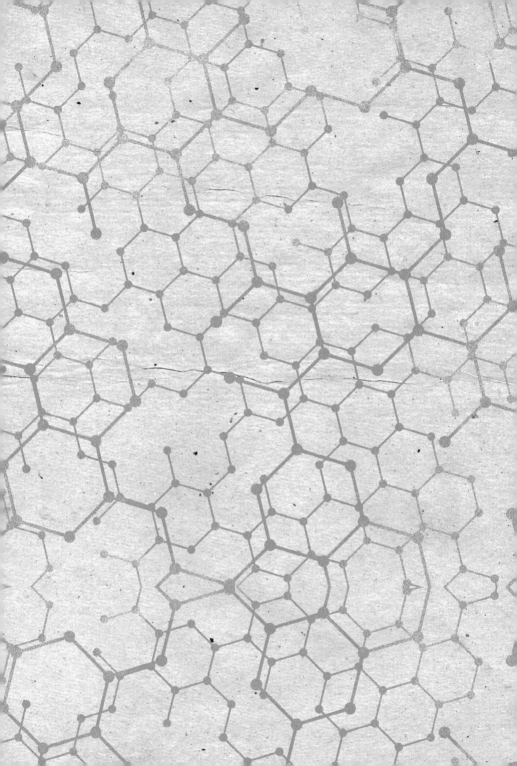

Further Exploration

The following websites were helpful to me while writing this book and are likely to remain active and helpful to teachers and learners in the years to come.

The Scientific Method (Chapter 1)

http://kids.nceas.ucsb.edu/DataandScience/index.html

https://www.sciencebuddies.org/science-fair-projects/science-fair/steps-of-the-scientific-method

http://www.sciencefun.org/kidszone/experiments/

Birds (Chapter 1)

http://www.birds.cornell.edu/

http://www.birdsleuth.org/

https://kids.nationalgeographic.com/animals/hubs/birds/

Genetics (Chapter 2)

https://history.nih.gov/exhibits/genetics/kids.htm

https://www.amnh.org/explore/ology/genetics

https://www.genome.gov/pages/education/modules/basicspresentation_vs2.pdf

Mendel's Peas (Chapter 2)

https://www2.edc.org/weblabs/Mendel/MendelMenu.html

https://www2.palomar.edu/anthro/mendel/mendel_1.htm

https://www.sciencelearn.org.nz/resources/2000-mendel-s-principles-of-inheritance

Punnett Squares (Chapter 2)

https://askabiologist.asu.edu/punnett-squares

http://www.biology.arizona.edu/mendelian_genetics/problem_sets/monohybrid_cross/01t.html

https://www.learner.org/interactives/dna/punnettsquare/

Geology (Chapter 3)

http://www.onegeology.org/extra/kids/rocks_and_minerals.html

https://www.learner.org/interactives/rockcycle/change3.html

https://www.nps.gov/tica/learn/education/upload/Erosion-Lab.pdf

Earth's Tilt (Chapter 4)

https://spaceplace.nasa.gov/seasons/en/

http://earthsky.org/earth/can-you-explain-why-earth-has-four-seasons

https://askabiologist.asu.edu/sites/default/files/resources/activities/earth-tilt/earths_tilt_activity_packet.pdf

Shadows (Chapter 4)

https://www.nasa.gov/audience/forstudents/k-4/stories/F_Keeping_Cool_With_Shadows.html

https://www.exploratorium.edu/snacks/colored-shadows

http://www.kean.edu/~fosborne/resources/ex11a1.htm

Gravity (Chapter 5)

https://spaceplace.nasa.gov/what-is-gravity/en/

http://idahoptv.org/sciencetrek/topics/gravity/facts.cfm

http://www.primaryscience.ie/media/pdfs/col/gravity_activity.pdf

The Moon (Chapter 5)

https://moon.nasa.gov/about/in-depth/

http://www.planetsforkids.org/moon-moon.html

http://nineplanets.org/luna.html

Tides (Chapter 5)

https://scijinks.gov/tides/

https://earthobservatory.nasa.gov/IOTD/view.php?id=90381

https://climatekids.nasa.gov/tidal-energy/

Acknowledgments

A huge thank you to Jonathan Eaton and the staff at Tilbury House Publishers for believing in this project. Thank you to Holly Hatam for capturing Acadia's journal with her beautiful illustrations.

My husband, Andrew, can be seen throughout these stories by those who know him. He gave feedback and ideas from the first draft through the final revisions. Thank you for the support you show me and the support you always give our family.

Thank you to my grown-up beta readers Andrew McCullough, Lindsay Coppens, and Peggy Becksvoort. Each of you brought a unique lens that made the book better. Thank you to my kid beta readers Greta Holmes, Sylvia Holmes, Isabel Carr, Allison Smart, and Greta Niemann for your honest (and very fun to read!) feedback. And thank you to my students at Falmouth Middle School; the sorts of questions you ask were with me as I wrote the stories and created a vision for Acadia's notebook.

And last but certainly not least, thank you to my fact checkers who helped edit and review the accuracy of the scientific content: Andrew McCullough, Grant Tremblay, Elise Tremblay, Sarah Dawson, Eli Wilson, Jean Barbour, and Bernd Heinrich, who generously answered a question no one else could. A lot of minds and a lot of knowledge are behind this book. I couldn't have done it without them.

Brendan Bullock

KATIE COPPENS lives in Maine with her husband and two children. She is an award-winning middle school language arts and science teacher. Much inspiration from this book came from her marriage to a high school biology teacher and from their focus on raising children instilled with compassion, curiosity, and creativity. Katie's publications include a teacher's guide for the National Science Teachers Association, *Creative Writing in Science: Activities That Inspire,* and she is a columnist for the NSTA's magazine *Science Scope..* She welcomes you to visit her at *www.katiecoppens.com.*

Children's book illustrator and graphic designer HOLLY HATAM (Whitby, Ontario) loves to combine line drawings, photography, and texture to create illustrations that pack energy and personality. Her picture books include *What Matters* (SONWA children's awards honorable mention) and the *New York Times* bestsellers *Dear Girl* and *Dear Boy*.

Tilbury House Publishers
Thomaston, Maine
www.tilburyhouse.com

Text © 2018 by Katie Coppens
Illustrations © 2018 by Holly Hatam

Hardcover ISBN 978-0-88448-601-5
Paperback ISBN 978-0-88448-602-2

10 9 8 7 6 5 4 3 2 1

Library of Congress Control Number: 2018932139

Cover and interior designed by Holly Hatam and Frame25 Productions
Printed in Canada